Feeling Dirty?
Life as a Laundromat Owner

About The Author:

Ken Barrett grew up on a farm outside Brooklin, Ontario, Canada. After a career in the auto industry he moved to the United States and now owns a chain of successful Laundromats in the South-East.

He has been featured in magazines, newspapers and articles for the speed of his store openings, attention to customer service and support of small businesses.

Marketing has become an interest and a passion and has allowed him a channel to provide a clear explanation of items that impact small businesses and Laundromats in particular.

During his careers he has worked as an Industrial Electrician, Project Manager, Quality Control Technician, Firefighter and Home Energy Advisor.

Ken now lives in Alabama with his wife, three daughters and two dogs. His main role at home is "The Transporter".

Ken Barrett
Ken@KBarInc.com

f FACEBOOK

Facebook.com/TheRealKBarrett

For More Information Please Visit
LaundromatHowTo.com

Feeling Dirty? Life as a Laundromat Owner.

For Information contact:

K-Bar Inc
829 Quintard Avenue
Anniston, AL
36201

ISBN 9781507626689

*This book is dedicated to all that have helped
and supported me through my journey
and to my wife, Trina, for her continued support and
encouragement.*

Table Of Contents

Recession Proof?

Many people look at Laundromats or Coin Laundry's as a recession proof business. Funny thing is nobody thought of them like that before 2008. They were just that place that poor people and college students go to wash their clothes because they can't afford a washer at home. Previous to 2008 the economy was doing great, money was easy to get, Laundromats were being built all over the place and nobody could see anything but money. A few years later and entire stores were being repossessed.

A Laundromat, like any business, needs customers. If you have the "build it and they will come" attitude you better have some deep pockets in case they don't. There are many pieces of the pie to go around and sometimes you can make the pie bigger but there are factors that may make the pie smaller as well.

Well run Laundromats with extra services can expand the pie from a traditional unattended Laundromat but changes in demographics will also make a difference to your business either up or down. We will get into some of the different issues later but now it's time for some of my background.

My Background

Let me start with my background and It's nothing to do with coin laundry's but I hope it helps with understanding how I look at and approach some of the items.

I was raised on a farm and went to college for two years and graduated from the Electrical Engineering Technician program. I just wanted to be an electrician but none of the counselors in my high school had any idea how to provide direction if it didn't involve post secondary education. So off I went to continue my education. As things like this normally work it put me into a job with a major automotive manufacturer just as they were building their first plant in the country. I started in production but soon moved into a robot operator role due to, you guessed it, my post secondary education. A few years there and I was able to get an apprenticeship as an Industrial Electrician where I spent the next 10 years repairing equipment.

Over the following 13 years I was involved in a number of projects that included supporting installation of new robotics, reducing utility consumption, building new factories, Safety and Quality Control.

In my spare time I was always working on projects around the house from finishing basements to building a log home.

After I left the corporate world in 2009, fortunately mine was by choice, I spent a few months as a Certified Energy Advisor working as an independent contractor.

This involved doing evaluations of people's homes for energy use including the Blower Door Test to check for leaks. This was a great job. It allowed me to combine something that interested me, use my past experience in home renovations to help people understand how their home worked, help them get government rebates for improvements and I actually got paid to do it.

This was a short career as I had my paperwork submitted to move to the US. I investigated the energy evaluation business in the US but found in the SouthEast it was not a big concern to most people and as there were very few rebate programs in place so the payback was from the energy savings only. Part of the difference in the attitude between the colder climates and the SouthEast is that you don't notice a warm breeze coming under a door with the air conditioning running but you definitely notice a cold breeze in the North.

As my time to move started to draw closer I continued to investigate various business opportunities. This was mainly in an effort to avoid going back to the corporate world. One of the businesses was coin laundries. No inventory. No employees. Somewhat passive income.
.

Years earlier I was introduced to the coin laundry industry by a friend of mine on our volunteer fire department. As he was a captain at the Fire Department and also did service on appliances he earned the title of Captain Freon. His family had been in the coin laundry and appliance sales and service business his whole life.

We would sit around and talk about various business ventures and at one point we actually took a tour of a couple of laundry's in a neighboring town. I had other projects on the go at the time so another friend of his opened one in that town a couple of years later.

Fast forward a few years and I had left the corporate world , and was getting ready to leave that country. Part of the fun of moving to the US is that once you are here it takes months to get a green card to be able to work but fortunately you can own a business before you even get here.

During the time I was waiting to move I hunted down Captain Freon and started asking questions. I would ride with him to his coin laundries and ask all kinds of questions about income and finance and maintenance and setup ……. Finally he told me until you actually own one I can't really tell you much more.

I will be honest and tell you that you can read about them, stop by and use some, talk to distributors, accountants and lawyers, develop business plans and study demographics but there are still things that you don't find out until you own one. But I hope to be able to provide some insight into many of these items as we move along.

I have been operating in the laundry business since 2010 and learning and studying since 2009. As I mentioned above during this time I was able to spend hours and days doing research. Currently I own 3 stores. One was closed and required a complete renovation, one was running and needed some freshening up and the third was running and had good equipment but needed renovations and some additional equipment. One of my stores has attendants and a strong Drop Off service. Although not in my original business plan it was a good opportunity so I made some adjustments to the business plan and moved forward.

Throughout this time I was also involved in marketing in many forms. Internet, newspapers, radio, TV and even billboards. I try to take two or three courses per year on business and marketing. Some are only a few hours at the local Chamber of Commerce or the University and some full day courses. I also invest a lot of time in on-line training, webinars and audio books.

There is no such thing as staying in the same place. You either move up or move down. This applies to business and personal activities. Staying in the same place actually means you are falling behind as everyone else moves ahead.

Coin Laundry Basics

If you have bought this book and read this far I am going to assume that you have an interest in the business and you are trying to figure out where to start.

The Coin Laundry business, like any other business, has its own terminology and metrics for determining how a business is doing.

Coin laundries are a destination business. Nobody is going to be driving down the street and be convinced to turn in and do their laundry because someone is standing by the side of the road spinning a sign. Although I did have someone follow me to the store because he saw the signs on my truck. Fortunately for me I was actually headed to the store.

Why do people need Laundromats and who are they?

No equipment at home: This can be due to an economic issue, equipment breakdown, moving or lack of space or hookups in their home or apartment.

Large Items: Comforters, large blankets, sleeping bags. These are all items that cannot be washed in home laundry equipment. Many will try and then they will carry the soaked comforter to your store to wash and dry in the right sized machine.

No Time: People that have washers and dryers at home may find that they just don't have enough time to run three or four loads of laundry. Typically a home washer will have a cycle time of 25 to 30 minutes and the dryer cycle time of 45 minutes. With loading and unloading that could take 4 to 5 hours to finish the laundry. The same amount at a Laundromat would take under an hour.

Transitional Workers: Many types of construction, farming, storm cleanup crews, pipeline workers and others are considered transitional workers. They may be in the area for a few days, weeks or months and then move on with the work. Or they may be seasonal. These workers tend to travel lightly and are always ready to move. Many times they stay in camper trailers at the local campground. They usually do not have laundry equipment and the equipment supplied at the campgrounds may not be suitable for a large volume of work clothes.

Demographics

Remember when the Census forms arrived in the mail and you complained about filling them out and how it just seemed like a waste of time, money and paper. All that data that gets gathered, sorted and filed is now going to be a major factor in determining the location and size of your laundry. Renters, homeowners, family size, income, age, background. These are all factors that will determine if you laundry even has a chance of survival.

Equipment Size

Home equipment is sold based on loads. Single load, double load etc. This is how the public describes and understands washer size. The laundry business refers to equipment based on pounds. A load of laundry is considered to be 10 pounds. So washer descriptions may be 18 pounds, 30 pounds, 55 pounds etc.

Dryers/ tumblers are also described in pounds. Most common sizes are 30 pound or 45 pound. They are also described by the number of pockets and may be single pocket or stacked. Stacked allows more pockets in the same amount of floor space. If the floor space is available single pockets dryers are more ergonomically friendly. At least one stacked drier may be required under the Americans With Disabilities Act (ADA). This may not apply in other countries.

Turns Per Day

The most basic description is how many cycles per day each piece of equipment runs. One cycle/ turn is equal to one paid wash load. The normal target number is three turns per day. This is based on a weekly average. If you have less than three turns per day you may not make enough to pay all the bills and you probably have too much equipment. More than three turns per day means that you may be backed up at busy times but should not be a problem unless you start to reach 5 turns per day. This is a total average for all machines so some may be used 5 or 6 times per day and others only during busy times.

Income Per Square Foot

In most Laundromats only about 25% of your floor space is income producing. The other areas are storage rooms, utility areas, folding tables, chairs, walkways etc. If you can negotiate a good lease payment this factor is not as important. Many laundries pack in the equipment and have too few folding tables or walkways.

Collections

This is the act of moving the money or tokens from the equipment to the change machine and collecting the cash for deposit. This is the part that most people think about, or dream about. One thing to keep in mind, It takes time to count the money and make the bank deposits. Although not a bad chore somebody has to do it and it has to happen to keep the store running. This may be two or three times per week. If you plan on taking a couple of weeks for a vacation you need someone you **trust** to do this job.

Types Of Laundromats And Services

Early in the planning stages of entering the Laundromat Industry you need to make a few decisions about your business model and the lifestyle you are looking for. There are a few types of Laundromats and they each have a different level of involvement and challenges.

Unattended Laundromats

These Laundromats have no staff at the store. Usually there is a cleaning company or individual that will clean the store once or twice a day or overnight.

Partially Attended Laundromats

Attendants are on duty for some of the hours during the day.

Fully Attended Laundromats

Attendants and/or management are at the store for all hours that the store is open.

NOTE: If you are considering hiring Employees a copy of my Employee Manual is available at http://www.laundromathowto.info

Drop Off Service (Fluff and Fold)

The Laundromat provides a service for the customer to drop off their clothes, comforters or other items for cleaning by the staff. Normally this involves separating the clothes, basic spot treating, washing, drying, folding and packaging.

Self Serve

The customer does all of the laundry themselves. The store may be attended, partially attended or unattended. If there are attendants they are there to help customers with the machine operation, cleaning and general customer support.

Full Service

A Full Service Laundry will offer a Drop Off Service, possibly Dry Cleaning, alterations, pick-up and delivery and other services.

Commercial Service

This is a B2B (Business To Business) service. Salons, Spa's, MRI clinics, and other small, local businesses usually don't have the quantity to use one of the big laundry supply companies. Local Laundromats are able to fill this niche market and provide more personal service.

My Business Model

When I first began looking into the Industry one of the appeals was that there were no employees, no inventory, and the customer paid for the service before receiving anything. Part of this was based on conversations with another owner and I still use this part of the business model- "I won't pay somebody to watch someone else do their laundry".

When a Laundromat became available in the same city as another of my stores I had to make some slight changes to my Business Plan. The store had a strong Drop Off Service but was run 12 hours a day, 7 days a week by the owner.

So it had to become a Partially Attended store but their main focus is the Drop Off Laundry Service. They are still expected to provide excellent customer service to everyone and maintain the store but their wages are paid by the Drop Off Division.

As a side note there are hundreds of Laundromats that are Full or Partially Attended and that is the business plan they work with. Store Size and Customer Volume should be the main determining factors as wage costs can quickly become a large portion of expenses.

Missing Coin Box

One of my unattended stores has a couple of large washers. Depending on the week the coin boxes were filling up between normal visits. As I was trying to determine my best options I would stop in occasionally to empty about 4 of the boxes.

I would pull out the first box, and dump the others into it and carry the box to the changer. The changer is wall mounted so I had to go into the back room to access it. It only took a few minutes and I was done.

On two occasions I came back to the store for my normal collections and found I had left the coin box in the back room. I'm sure there were some customers that realized they could get a $6 wash for free by just catching the quarters but on both occasions I found $6 in the refund box with a note that said " I noticed the box was missing but I owe you for the wash.

Payment Systems

Paying to do your laundry used to be so simple. You put in the quarters and pressed start. Now there are many methods for payment in Laundromats and more are being developed at a lightning pace.

The location of your laundry will have some determination on the payment methods used. A Laundromat in downtown New York is going to have a different clientele then a small town in Alabama. They still have the same basic needs for a Laundromat but some areas are more used to credit and debit and never carry cash. I was in one of my Laundromats having a discussion about payment systems and mentioned card systems. A customer overheard us talking and said "If I can't use cash I'll be going someplace else". How's that for honest customer feedback!

Cash

Currently, and possibly always, is King. The denominations are changing as the prices rise but in the US the quarter is still the main method to make a coin operated washer start.

Many machines are being equipped for dollar coins to reduce the number of coins needed to start the machine and thereby reduce the amount of collections needed. As shown in another post I have had to modify my coin boxes to allow them to hold more quarters. It was the best, low cost, quick solution available

Will dollar coins replace bills in the US like they

have in many other countries? It may take awhile but it is probably inevitable. Canada has had $1 coins for over 20 years and has recently announced that it has stopped making pennies. Cash transactions are rounded up or down to the nearest nickel but debit and credit transactions are conducted at the exact amount

Tokens

Similar concept to using cash. It has the advantage of keeping the cash out of the public areas as well as being used in promotions and refunds. Coin acceptors are available that can handle quarters, dollars and tokens. There is an upfront cost to getting the tokens as you may want to have them custom made with your logo and information. The tokens will only work in your store (or stores). There is a replacement cost due to unused tokens but the customer paid you for them already.

Laundry Cards

These are specific to your store (s). Money is added through a Value Transfer Station that will accept cash, credit or debit. The amount of the wash or dry is removed from the card when each machine is started. There are some differences between systems that allow you to track and replace the value on lost cards if a customer has added their contact information which also allows you to monitor the activity of your customers and identify the large volume, frequent and long term customers.

Credit / Debit Cards

These are being accepted directly at the washers and dryers. Some systems will still allow coins or tokens to be used as well. They can be added to a few machines at a time and usually connect through a secure, wireless router. This eliminates individual wiring of the machines to the central location and expanding the system requires little effort.

Kiosks

The washers and dryers are started from a central location and the total amount is paid in cash or by debit or credit card at that location. These are in addition to the normal coin acceptor on the machine so if there is a problem with the kiosk or system the machines can still be run with cash at each location.

Near Field Communication

Microchips in credit and debit cards and some smart phones transfer the amount of payment when it is in close proximity to the payment device on the washer or dryer. I was recently on a trip to Canada and found these are common on all credit card devices in stores and restaurants. The merchants I used stumbled a little when my US card had to be swiped.

The type of payment method you install will be based on your local area and the amount of investment you have available. This decision is not always given the attention it deserves. Changing payment systems is costly as each piece of equipment must be considered from the biggest washer to the vending and change machines. The right components installed initially may allow changes without complete replacement.

If you have or are purchasing an existing store that has a variety of machines from different manufacturers and years it may be difficult to convert everything to a particular system.

Other factors will include if you or your staff are comfortable emptying cash from the individual washers or if you want to keep all of the cash in a secure area. Does your customer base use debit or credit cards? Will you be offering a Drop Off Service where your attendants will need to start the same washers and dryers as the customers?

Integrated payment systems provide an almost unlimited amount of business monitoring and feedback. You will be able to determine the busiest times in your store, what machines are used the most and other information that will assist in future planning.

Additional features allow prices to be changed based on day of week and time of day so you can offer lower prices on slow days , traditionally Tuesday and Wednesday. This allows seniors and others with flexible time to be moved away from your busy times and be compensated for it.

Customers can also be given discounts or bonuses when they add value to their card. For example if they add

$100 to their card $120 is put on. This secures your customer for an additional amount of time using your store and they receive a benefit.

One concern with this system is the operation of your store is dependent on the system operating. At an attended store you may be able to train your staff to reset and/ or troubleshoot the system but at an unattended store you will need to deal with it when it happens.

Cards and tokens do provide the benefit of allowing you to offer prizes and other benefits in an unattended store.

The Roof Leak

It was a dark and stormy night and the next day started with a text message and a picture. "Part of the ceiling fell in." Fortunately it was only part of one ceiling tile. Once I got to the store I found out it was right over the kids area so I grabbed the ladder and pulled down the soaked tile and insulation and found two leaks.

Let me give you some history on the roof of my store. I lease 1600 ft2 in a strip mall that has a total of about 25,000 ft2. The building was originally a grocery store in the large part of the mall. After a few years an addition was put on that included the Laundromat. This was all done in the '70's. Over the years things changed in the mall and the big area had been split into an auto parts store and a furniture rental store. The Laundromat continued to run with the same old equipment and the end unit beside the laundry was a franchise sandwich shop. The two big tenants moved out to their own buildings and the landlord ran out the leases on the Laundromat and sandwich shop and didn't renew them. This left him with an empty building on a valuable piece of Real Estate on a main road in front of the hospital and then the economy slowed down in the area and then the rest of the country. The owner of the property sold and the new owner decided to fill the building instead of tearing it down. My Laundromat was the first tenant back into the building in 2010.

From the start we had issues with roof leaks as the roof was original and basically a tar paper type layer over a material that looks like fat fiberglass fibres. The landlord rolled some patch material on it but anytime somebody walks on it there is a leak of some type, many times from any screws, stones or debris left from various contractors. About a year after we opened the roof seemed to be patched enough to work.

In 2012 the large areas of the building were being renovated for a Social Security Office and a lawyer's office. They tore off all the old HVAC equipment and got ready for the new roof. I asked the property manager if I would be getting a new roof as well. He had a simple answer, "No".

In 2013 the final part of the building, the end unit beside the Laundromat was being renovated for a credit company. I dove up one day and saw a roofer's truck and some guys carrying stuff up the ladder. I asked if they were doing the roof on the laundry too. Simple answer "No".

It would appear that while they were working on the new roof over the credit company they stepped over the line onto the Laundromat roof which brings us to the current leaks. I sent a text to the property manager and he said they would send somebody when it stopped raining.

After I pulled down the tile and insulation I grabbed a couple of buckets and put them under the leak. Next step was to use some cardboard to block off the entrance to the kids area so no one would get injured or move the buckets.

Another leak was in a back room behind the change machine and right beside the security camera DVR, WiFi and cable box. I move some things out of the way, taped some plastic around the electronics and taped a piece of tile board over the change machine to deflect any water from it. I opened up the hole a little and put a mop bucket under it.

Next was a stop to the other store where a found the scale we use for the Drop Off Service was causing problems. I called the manufacturer and was able to make it get it back online. I ordered another one so we can send it for repairs.

The next day the rain had stopped and I was able to install a new ceiling tile and open the kids area for business.

Customer Experience

This is a key part of today's Laundromats. Customers are not just looking for a place to Wash and Dry their clothes. They expect to have enough space, be entertained and be comfortable.

Folding Tables

In the laundry industry this means a table to fold the laundry on, not a table that folds up.

Folding tables do not make money in a laundry, they take up a lot of space and people sit on them every day, so why have them?

While there are many people that take their laundry from the dryer and stuff it straight into the bag or even fold them straight from the dryer (which has the result of reducing your dryer availability for other customers), the majority of people want to get everything folded and stacked so it's ready to put away when they get home.

As a laundry owner the folding tables are a convenience item like the TV's and Wifi, they provide a better experience to meet your customers needs.

There are many sizes, colors and materials available for folding tables. The traditional table is made of fiberglass. The sides and back have a raised, rounded edge to prevent clothes from falling on the floor or being pushed onto another table. Some stores use stainless steel tables and other materials are beginning to show up on the market.

A decent sized table will cost you a few hundred dollars but will last for years. These tables will be sat on, stood on, pushed around, spilled on and anything else you can imagine. Some tables allow a pole to be added on the front corners for hangers and shelves over the back of the table for more storage area of folded clothes.

Avoid shelves and supports under the tables as this space will be used to store laundry carts, garbage cans and maybe a chair or two.

Recently I have seen an innovative setup that works well. The dryers are spaced out along the wall and the tables are built into the alcove between. As they are framed on 3 sides and covered with a durable material, in this case ceramic tile, they are very sturdy, cannot tip over or be moved and cost effective.

Whatever method, style or type you put in try to make them as large as possible. They need to be deep enough to allow folded clothes to be stacked along the back and still have room to fold more. I have found 24" table to be too narrow and prefer 30"+. A width of 5' to 6' also allows enough room to fold pants and towels with clothes stacked at the side.

Locations need to be determined when you store is laid out. Keep in mind the flow of the store between equipment and that people will be standing in front of the folding table for up to 30 or 40 minutes. If they are on a main aisle way there needs to be enough room for others to pass by. Being able to fold and watch TV helps your customers pass the time.

Table grouped together make a great place to fold blankets and comforters when they are all available.

I have seen some busy stores with very few places to fold and sometimes the size of the building and the equipment needed to generate the required revenue dictate that. As in a good restaurant sometimes people will just get takeout and finish at home if there aren't enough tables.

Wifi

As the use of laptops, tablets and Wifi enabled smartphones grows more people expect to be able to get free WiFi. Some places charge a minimum fee or require you to Like their social media page, which is a great way to build your audience, more details below on that.

Personally I love to use free Wifi and have been known to park outside the odd store or business to use a few minutes to get something done. Many people in the laundry will have a smartphone with a limited data package so they use WiFi whenever possible.

This is one of the first things I put in my stores. Mainly because I want to use it myself when I am there. You will need an internet connection for remote viewing of your cameras and for your cash register credit card acceptance so adding a wireless router with a Guest feature is not that difficult.

Some cable company agreements may actually prevent offering free unlimited Wi-Fi. Read your agreement and determine what restrictions you need to put in place. There are some companies that offer a free or paid service that can help you avoid any issues with your supplier. Typically they allow a customer to access the Wifi through Facebook, Google+ or a form sign up.

The benefit of these services is that you get traffic to your Facebook page as well as the analytic data of users.

From a customer point of view this is a great feature. I have some customers that don't have internet access at home so they use the one at the Laundromat, fast food restaurants and the library.

There are many routers that can be used to set up your WiFi. I like to use a good quality, "large home" router from any electronics store and prefer brand names. If you are setting up your own cameras you will have to make some changes in the router and support is usually available by phone. If you are using a company to setup your security cameras ask them to provide or recommend a router so it won't cause any issues when they arrive.

Your ability, or that of your camera installation contractor will play a role in the type of router you install.

I was finding that every few weeks my customers could not access the Wifi. I was able to on the secure side but the guests were not. I cycled the power on the router and that seemed to fix the problem. With that knowledge, and little else of the details of the problem I put a timer on the router power supply to turn it off for 15 minutes at 2am every day. I have not had any complaints since that time.

I mentioned above about routers that require your customer to "Like" your social network page to access free WiFi. This is done with a programmed router and an online support company. There is normally a fee for the service based on the number of "Likes" you are allowed per month. You customer may be given the option to "Like" your page for free access or pay for service. I would suspect most if not all will opt for the free access and they can always Unlike you later if they want to.

Overall my thoughts are that I would never open a location without offering free WiFi. There is a financial factor that must be considered as a business phone, cable and internet package may cost up to $200 or more a month depending on the options but it's part what I consider a necessary utility. If your competitors have free WiFi and you don't you are at a disadvantage already but if you have it and they don't it's another marketing tool you can promote.

Kids Area

Every Laundromat should have a kids area. It doesn't have to be big and stuffed with toys but there should be some defined place that the parents can send their kids. There are some things to keep in mind to keep you out of trouble. Make sure the area is kid proof. This goes for your whole store but kids are going to bang their heads on folding tables and dryer doors. In the kids area take the time to think about how it will be used. There will be 2 year old kids in there and 14 year old kids.

I like to build a bit of a corral. I frame a four foot high wall with 2x4's and cover it with plywood. Usually it is against a building wall that is drywall so I will cover that with a sheet of MDF and chalkboard paint. A key ingredient is the TV. I usually use a 27" TV and mount it in a recessed box in one of the plywood walls. The cable and power plugs are also in the recess. I cover it with a clear piece of Lexan or other tough, clear plastic. Drill some holes in the top and bottom edges to allow airflow to keep the TV cool. (expect to get chalk, lollipop sticks, gum wrappers and anything else that can fit in the holes in there. Screw it around the outside with a few different type screws. You may want to use a torx and allen head as well. This reduces the chance of theft.

Another option I like to add is windows. These are usually bought at a Habitat For Humanity Restore or from the extras bin at a building supply store. The windows are mounted on the outside wall and the inside is covered with Lexan. This eliminates a ledge that the kids can climb on. I have two different size chairs that I bought from a school supply company. I tried the wooden table and chair set but they lasted about 3 weeks until the older kids started tilting back on them.

My thoughts on the kids area design was to provide a safe place, with some entertainment, for the kids to hang out. They have their own chairs and a TV set to a kids channel and chalk board. They can look out the windows and see what's going on in the Laundromat. The opening to the kids area is away from the front door so it makes it more difficult for them to make a break for it when somebody opens the door.

For the parents they have a "place" to send the kids to, it's easy for them to look over the top and see what the kids are doing and they can relax and watch the other TV's or talk to friends.

Some items to keep in mind: Supplying toys , especially in an unattended laundry will probably lead to them disappearing. There is also the chance that a kid may step on something or chew on something and get injured. This will point back to you and your business for providing the toys. Attended Laundromats will have less problems with this. If your store is partially attended then make sure you have a policy to put the toys away during off hours.

I will try and pick up kids books where ever I can, yard sales, book stores, department stores. Many are under a dollar and at some yard sales you can get a box for a few dollars. Leave a few out at a time. They will eventually get torn up and thrown out and some kids might take them home. I don't mind this as it may be the only book they have. I had one little boy wearing a Spiderman shirt and carrying a stuffed Spiderman wanted the new Spiderman book I had just put out. How could I turn down that request?

Laundry Carts

There are a few formulas for how many laundry carts you need to provide. At the very least one per folding table is a good start. A mixture of carts with and without poles should be provided as some people will bring hangers and want to be able to hang their clothes as they take them from the baskets. Carts without poles are easily stored under the tables and don't get in the way when opening washer and dryer doors. There is some basic maintenance required to clean the threads and hair out of the wheels and some of these carts will get stolen in unattended and partially attended Laundromats.

Seating

Customers will be in your store for up to an hour or more. Although many people will sit in their cars or outside or may even leave while their items are in the machines there are always customers sitting in the store. Any seating provided needs to be tough and easy to clean. Fiberglass, painted steel and plastic are the main types. Some stores will use bench seating others may use round tables with fixed seating like many fast food restaurants, and I have even seen leather recliners. These decisions all need to take into account your available space, clientele , and focus area (TV's for example).

Power Outlets

Almost everybody has a laptop, tablet or cell phone and if you have WiFi then they will be using them in the store so you should provide some outlets for recharging these items. When placing them in the store keep in mind that people may still be using the device while it is plugged in. I would recommend that you don't have any receptacles near you folding tables. This will prevent customers from using the folding tables as a desk and they will not be available for other customers. The receptacle need to be on their own circuits so if they are overloaded and trip the breaker they will not affect any equipment. I would also recommend they be protected with a Ground Fault Interrupter (GFI) due to the possibility of water in the area. If you have a covered store front you may even consider receptacles on the outside of the store. This will allow people who may be smoking to charge their devices as well. A timer could be installed to turn the receptacle off after hours.

The amount of power used by your customers for these receptacles will be minor compared to your total power bill but are a great benefit to your customers.

Lighting

Lighting has changed from florescent T-12 to T-8 and some T-5. Now the switch is to LED.

From a cost saving point the LED is the best method to use at this point. The power consumption, and lack of repairs and maintenance more than makes up for any front end costs. The cost of legally disposing of florescent tubes could justify the cost itself.

My current stores have not been converted to LED's at this point. One advantage of the florescent actually has to do with the Laundry Detergent. The soap contains Optical Brighteners that make clothes look brighter and cleaner under florescent lighting. One reason clothes in stores and at Laundromats always look better than at home.

Another method I have employed at the store is to use different temperature bulbs based on location. The higher the temperature the "whiter" the light. With this in mind I use 4100K bulbs over the folding tables and 3200k bulbs in other areas. This provides a softer light in the seating and kids areas.

Store Supplies

What are the essentials to have around your store? There are a number of items that you will need around your laundry. These items are not things used as part of your Drop Off service but are just used for basic store cleaning and maintenance. Some may change depending on what type of cleaning service you use. Some companies will provide all of their own supplies and equipment and transport them to the store each day. If you are hiring someone local or using your attendants you will need to provide a storage room for supplies and equipment. This room will need a place to fill a mop bucket, preferably with hot water, and empty the bucket.

Supplies will include floor cleaner, window cleaner, a general surface cleaner, toilet cleaners and stainless steel cleaner and polish. I have found using washcloths for cleaning will save you money over using paper or disposable towels. These can be washed and dried at the store and you will build your supply with cloths that are left in the washers and dryers. I avoid any cleaners with bleach in them, this prevents any residue from being left on a table or washer surface and damaging someone's clothes.

Anther item you should keep in the store is a step ladder. I have a 6 foot one that does everything I need. A Wet / Dry vacuum and some basic hand tools are always helpful. Many of the small issues that come up can be fixed with a couple of screwdrivers, small socket set and a crescent wrench.

Security

Laundromats have a bad reputation by many as being unsafe, dirty and not a place that they really want to go but must go. Providing security for your store and customers is required and may be mandatory for your insurance coverage.

Cameras

There are very few places you can go that you are not being recorded or viewed by security cameras. These may be personal, business , police or municipality, State or Federal owned but they are there. Cameras in a Laundromat are not optional. As a minimum you need to have camera coverage on your change machine, preferably from a couple of angles (this is also good to be able to monitor the "Out Of Order" light from your phone), front door and if possible the parking lot, the inside of the front door and a general view of the laundry. If you have attendants you need to cover the cash register and if you offer a drop off service I suggest having a camera in the sorting area as well.

Having a few hidden cameras all always a good option. Some vandals in one of my stores were caught due to their car being seen by a hidden camera that was mounted lower than the visible camera. Know how to review your cameras and how much storage space is available on your DVR. The more cameras, the less time that is recorded.

Do not use fake or dummy cameras. This can cause a problem if there is a situation in your store and you are only providing the "illusion" of security. In the overall cost of a Laundromat this is one of the cheapest items you will buy but it will be priceless if you have a confrontation between an employee and a customer or you have some vandalism.

In my experience dealing with a few acts of vandalism and some theft, report all issues to the Police no matter how small. You may not be claiming them on your insurance but this allows the Police to get video and pictures and if they are caught in a number of locations or are repeat offenders it will help build a case against them. Some vandals at one of my stores were caught and admitted to trying to rob every Carwash and Laundromat in a 30 mile area but there was no other reports made to any Police Departments.

Bottom Line: Install good cameras and know how to use them.

Door Locks

Running a 24 hours store or on based on certain hours will determine the method of locking your store. Other factors will include the locations.

I have tried a few methods. Store 1 and 3 used electric door locks. These allowed the doors to be unlocked at a set time. The doors would lock at night and anyone in the store could exit past that time but not get back in. Shortly after the doors locked the lights turned off part of the store at a time until only a couple were left on. These stores have since been switched to 24 hours so the locks are not used.

Store 2 was manually locked and unlocked by the cleaner. This method is used by others I know in their locations. It has the advantage of making sure no one is spending the night in the store bit the person cannot lock the door until everyone is gone. One of the problems I had was unlocking in the morning. My cleaner could not get there until after the school bus picked up her kids at 7:45. Whenever I was there earlier I noticed people were coming in so I switched this store to 24 hours as well.

Alarm Systems

Alarm systems are a must for any laundry. The areas covered by the alarm may vary. If you are running a 24 hour store you don't need to put alarms in the public areas but having an alarm on the secure areas is a good plan.

There are many options available. You can have a big name company install an entire system including cameras and have video monitoring of the store. If there is an alarm they will look at the cameras and call the required people. If you are not open 24 hours they can check the cameras to make sure the store is empty before turning on the alarms. Another option is to buy the systems and install them yourself. Keep in mind if you install them it means you troubleshoot and repair them as well.

There are many accessories beside the cameras, motion and door sensors.

Water Sensors- A couple of these are a good idea. They will detect water on the floor. Put them in an area, usually in a bulkhead, where they will not come into contact with floor mops. I have two sensors, one behind a bulkhead in about the middle of the store and one in the janitor's closet.

Vibration Sensors- These can actually be put inside your change machine in case someone is attempting to remove the entire machine. We have all seen the news about people hooking a truck to an ATM and tearing it out of the store.

GPS Tracking- These are used to track a change machine that has been ripped out of your store. I prefer to have a wall mounted change machine to reduce the chance of it being towed away.

Secure Areas

These are the areas of the store that the public will not have access to. There are a couple of different areas and they should be kept separate. One area is the janitorial supplies. This is usually a small room with a laundry tub type sink and a place for pouring out a mop bucket. Supplies kept in this area are mops, brooms, bathroom supplies, ladders and step stools for cleaning the tops of the big washers, changing HVAC filters and changing light bulbs. We normally don't use paper towels for cleaning as rags can be washed and used for a long time. You will also find your rag supply grows over time as they are left in washers and dryers.

Another area is the access area behind the dryers. This area is not conditioned air meaning that it is not heated or cooled. The dryers need a lot of air and they pull from the back area. It tends to get dusty and is not normally used for storage.

The biggest area of concern is the secure area behind the change machines. This is where the money will be handled and is normally the location of the security camera DVR, WiFi, security system controls, safe and cable connections. This area needs to be difficult to get into from all sides and don't forget the top. These rooms are normally built with plywood. The customer side is then covered with drywall or tile board for a finished look. The doors are normally steel and are locked at all times and only trusted people should have access to the keys. A monitor for the security cameras should be available to check the area before leaving.

How the rooms are set up and accessed will be determined by your store layout but always review the construction, door types and locations before building or renovating. The goal is to prevent access to this area or slow a thief down enough for the police to arrive.

A Small Leak

I received a call from a customer at the store about some water leaking from a washer. I had a comment about this particular washer a few days before that there was a small leak from the door when it was running. This washer is a small soft mount, frontload washer that pumps the water to the drain, similar to a top loader. The caller said there was a small leak from the door and the customer using the machine managed to get the door open and there was water all over the floor. Many people have different versions of "all over the floor" and I had heard and seen most of them. I told her I would be over shortly.

I got to the store about two hours later and it appeared her version of "all over the floor" was very accurate. About 25% of the floor had water on it. I noticed the machine in question had been unplugged but mopping was first on the list.

About an hour and four mop buckets later I had the water cleaned up. Let's do some math. A mop bucket holds about 4 gallons of water, a small front load washer uses about 12 gallons of water for one wash and two rinses in a normal cycle. The washer was still full of water to the bottom edge of the door.

It seems that when the door was opened the washer was in a fill cycle and continued to fill as it wouldn't reach the full level with the door open. Someone unplugged the washer which would have closed the fill valve and stopped

the water flow.
One good thing, the floor was clean when I was done.

Floor Coverings

There are many options for floor coverings.

Commercial Vinyl Tile (CVT)

This is used in many types of stores including the big name stores. I have this in one of my stores and it looks good but requires maintenance. This type of floor requires waxing regularly and buffing. Usually only spot mopping is done and cleaners such as Pine Sol cannot be used. When it gets worn it must be stripped and waxed again. Due to the amount of dust and dirt in a Laundromat and baskets and hampers being dragged across the floor this is a poor choice of floor covering. Learn from my experience.

Tile

There are many types of floor tile. Porcelain, ceramic, slate and others. Each type has good and bad features that must be considered. The number one issue to consider is how slippery it is when it gets wet or has some soap on it. Next is how well does it clean and how easy it is to clean. Ceramic tile looks great and if laid wit very small grout lines is easy to clean but most are very slippery when wet.

Carpet

I put this in as it is not really an option although one of my Laundromats had carpet when I bought it. The bottom layer was a brown, commercial carpet from sometime in the 70's. On top of this one of the previous owners had laid 7' x 9' area rugs in whatever color was available. Brown, green, red, blue. Any edges that became loose or a trip hazard were taped down with duct tape. Te only advantage I saw for this was about 1 month before I bought the store when I was still negotiating with the owner I stopped by one morning in December and found a water pipe had frozen and cracked. Water was spraying across the store. I put a bucket over the pipe and began to look for the main shutoff. The owner had no idea where it was. After about 10 minutes I found a valve in the ceiling that shut off the water. The carpet managed to hold most of the water and only a small amount got under the wall and into the dining room of the caterers in the next unit. They moved some tables and carried on as I mopped the floor. The Laundromat owners spent the next 4 hours using shop vacs to dry the carpets.

Within about a week of taking over the store I began to remove the carpet. Each time the store was empty one of the area rugs would be rolled up, the carpet underneath was cut out, the sand was vacuumed up and the area rug was put back down. After a week or so I rolled up all of the area rugs and threw them out. That was probably one of the most noticeable and talked about changes I made. The store was a little noisier but was much easier to keep clean. The residual glue was scrapped off over the next couple of weeks.

All that being said there are some Laundromats that have carpet and have made it work.

Sealed Concrete

One of the easiest floor covering methods and the one I used in my store after the carpet was removed was just sealing the concrete. Unsealed concrete with continue to put of a slight dust as people walk over it and baskets are dragged across. Also unsealed concrete will absorb water making mopping almost impossible. Sealing the concrete is an easy process. As my concrete was very old and I only had one night to do it I used a single part, quick drying sealer. It was just rolled on like paint and left to dry. The problem with a quick drying sealer is it is very flammable and has a lot of fumes. And, as I found out, dries very slowly on a warm Alabama night.

Another method is a two-part epoxy which once set is very durable.

Stained Concrete

This is probably the best method for Laundromat floors. It allows you to put a pattern or color on the floor but is sealed afterwards to give you the durability and ability to clean. A small amount of fine sand can be put in the sealer to increase traction.

During the planning of your laundry construction or renovation look into the various methods, as always visit other Laundromats, get prices for different methods and make sure the method you choose is scheduled correctly. Although it is great to get the entire floor stained and sealed before any equipment goes in be prepared to repair any scratches to the surface. This should also be discussed with your equipment installer or distributor so they are aware of the conditions they will be working in. Tile needs to be installed after the equipment but dryers may need to be raised slightly to allow the lower screen to be removed for cleaning.

A final item is to have a carpet or runner outside and inside your door. This catches a lot of sand and dirt from being tracked in and reduces water at the entrance on a rainy day. You can purchase these with you Laundromat logo on them as well.

Store Layout and the Flow Of The Customer.

The layout of your store will have a big impact on your customer satisfaction and your income. People who are new to your laundry or people who prefer to stay out of the spotlight will go to the first washers they can find available. If your smallest washers are located at the front of your store to the right of the door they will get the most use. Instead of installing 20# washers by the door put in a row of 30# washers. These will provide more revenue from the same customers or they will walk deeper into your store to find the smaller washers. This will cause them to see the various size washers available as well as any other services you offer. If you have attendants it gives them a better chance to interact with customer.

People who are going to use the big washers are going to have a lot of items. Seems like a simple concept but they are coming to the Laundromat to wash a lot of clothes and spend a lot of money. They are going to be there for awhile so why make them carry all of their dirty clothes to the back of the store? Put the big washers at the front, straight inside the door and preferably where they can be seen from the road.

Each Laundromat will have a variety of washer sizes. No single size can accommodate your customers and having a good mix allows them to be the most efficient with their money. They may need a 60# machine for their blankets, a 50# machine for their darks and a 30# machine for their whites. Having a variety of machines available in close proximity allows your customers to load all their items easily, reduce time moving between machines filling soap and depositing the money and also reduces the chance of them forgetting a load and tying up your machine for an extended period.

You want to make sure that there is a nice visual flow to your laundry and having a 60# washer beside a 50# with a 30# on the other side and then the same again beside it would be very distracting and chaotic but installing the large washers on the end of an aisle and having different sizes on each side of the aisle near it allows the customers the variety they need in close proximity.

Designers of kitchens have used the Kitchen Work Triangle as a model for many years. The concept is that for a kitchen to flow efficiently the triangle between the sink, stove and fridge must be within a certain parameter. Not too close and not too far. This reduces the amount of walking required but allows enough room to work. When designing a laundry layout some of the same concepts need to be used.

Consider the customer when they come to the laundry. They will bring in their dirty clothes and detergents. This may be in one or a number of trips or they may have some help from their kids or your attendants. They place the baskets on the floor in front of the biggest machine they need. Usually their next step is to get the change they need. Experienced people know to do this in case they find the change machine out of order (which will not happen in your laundry because you have at least a couple of change machines).

They return to the washer and load all of the machines they need, put in the soap and softener and start the machines. This is the first time they have had to stop and really look around your store. And what are they looking for?

1- A place to sit down

2- Entertainment- TV, magazines, a Wifi signal.

3- Something for the kids to do. You will have kids in your laundry and they need something to do. I am willing to sacrifice some real estate for a kid's area. More details can be found on that in another section.

4- Snacks and drinks.

The next item on their list will be to start scouting for dryers. What is available, are their different sizes, is anybody finishing up. How far do I have to walk to get a dryer.

After all the loads are in the dryer and started they will take a break for a few minutes and then get ready to stake a claim on a folding table. This is usually done by moving to the table and leaning on it to watch the dryers, then laying a coat on it or putting a basket on it.

After the drying and folding are complete it all gets moved to the car. This normally takes more trips than when they arrived. (Not many people let their kids carry the clean clothes back out).

The last trip is for the kids, remaining drinks and snacks and a quick check of the dryers and table for lost items.

All laundry design has to consider a number of factors. Building size and layout, amount of equipment required to accommodate the volume of traffic in the store, income producing area (nobody makes money from a folding table) and customer experience. When you begin laying out your store keep these items in mind and walk through your store on paper as a customer would.

In one of my stores I reduced the amount of customer area, added dryers, reduced the number of top load washers, removed half of the folding tables, built a kids area and increased my revenue. The store flows better, the big washers are right inside the front door, the top loaders are in the back and there is lots of room in front of the dryers. I also replaced the 15" TV with a 32" and 42" and a 27" for the kids.

Insurance Issues

Like your car or your home you need to have good insurance that will provide the coverage you need for theft, vandalism, fire, injury and anything else you can think of. Business insurance is different than homeowners insurance and you need to review the coverage for each section. You may want to talk to other laundry owners, your distributor or your accountant to confirm you have the right amount. If you have a major fire you don't want to be in a situation where you can't rebuild the store completely or have to make the Lease payments from your own savings.

With the insurance you can also buy Terrorism Insurance. This is optional but taking it will depend on where your Laundromat is located and to an extent your own beliefs on society. I do have it on one of my stores but I am in a strip mall with a Federal Office and for the small amount of additional premium it gives me the peace of mind I want.

Coin Laundry Association

"The <u>Coin Laundry Association's</u> (CLA) mission is to ensure a profitable and growing retail, self-service laundry operation by providing superior education, products and services to laundry owners". The best place to learn about the coin laundry industry, purchase demographic information, host your website, get information from leaders in the Industry, ask questions and keep up to date on legislation affecting Laundromats.

The Clean Show

Even this Industry gets a Trade Show. Held Bi-annually in different locations around the US and Officially known as <u>The Laundry, Drycleaning and Textile Care Industry Trade Show</u> it brings all of the manufacturers and suppliers of everything related to getting clothes clean.

Giving

I was at one of my stores a few months back with a couple of my early teenage kids. As I was filling the change machine a lady entered the store and was loading up a couple of the washers. I gave each of the kids $2 in quarters and asked them to go over and pay for the lady's washers. They did this and we finished up and got in the car.

They were so amazed at how thankful the lady was for the free washes. One of the comments was "But it was only $2". I explained that you don't know the situation the lady is in. She may be having a hard time paying all the bills and getting the laundry done is tough or maybe she was having a bad day and that free wash was the break she needed to put a smile on her face.

Never underestimate the difference that a small donation of money or time can make.

I continue this at various times in all my stores. As someone is loading a machine I may run the washer price down to $1 or less and smile and say we are having a spot sale.

What's a Normal Day Like?

It's easier to look at my total week then just one day as I can move activities around. In a normal week I visit all of the stores but the time spent at each one varies.

One of the stores requires very little attention. On average I spend less than an hour a week there. The store is located 30 miles away and not near the other stores so drive time is a bigger factor. About once or twice a month I will spend 2-3 hours doing any repairs or maintenance that needs to be completed.

The other stores are closer to each other, although no closer to my house in a different direction. One is unattended and needs about an hour twice a week normally. The partially attended store has a good drop off business so more time is spent on ordering supplies, payroll, store promotions and general interaction with the attendants.

Many days of the week I will pick my kids up from school and take them to various activities. Doctors, dentists and all those other places that are hard to get to when you work "normal" hours never seem to be a problem for me.

I also attend Chamber of Commerce activities. This has helped build the Drop Off business by simply just meeting people and putting a face on the business. Once someone visits the store it's up to the attendants to provide the excellent customer service they do daily and the business builds through the strongest marketing available, Word of Mouth.

I do many of my own repairs and share the information on LaundromatHowTo.com as well as continue to look for new ways to promote Laundromats and other small businesses.

Why name the book "Feeling Dirty?"

Below is a billboard that I used when I opened my first Laundromats.

Conclusion

This is really not the conclusion as the business continues on. I am always learning more and passing on information to other new or potential business owners.

There have been some frustrating times in this business and many laughs as well. I have met hundreds of great people and customers that appreciate the services we offer and the pride we take in our stores.

Owning and running a successful Laundromat has some challenges but many more rewards.

Ken Barrett
Multi-Store Laundry Owner

Ken@WashinCoinLaundry.com

in LINKEDIN   f FACEBOOK

For More Information Please Visit
LaundromatHowTo.com

-----------------------------THE END----------------------------
(For Now)

www.ingramcontent.com/pod-product-compliance
Lightning Source LLC
Chambersburg PA
CBHW070931180526
45168CB00003B/1031